New Beginnings Understanding Fostering

Saba Asghar

New Beginnings Understanding Fostering

Author: Saba Asghar

Copyright © 2025 Saba Asghar

The right of Saba Asghar to be identified as author of this work has been asserted by the author in accordance with section 77 and 78 of the Copyright, Designs and Patents Act 1988.

ISBN 978-1-83538-549-4 (Paperback)
      978-1-83538-550-0 (Hardback)
      978-1-83538-551-7 (E-Book)

Book Cover Design and Book Layout by:
    Maple Publishers
    www.maplepublishers.com

Published by:
    Maple Publishers
    Fairbourne Drive, Atterbury,
    Milton Keynes,
    MK10 9RG, UK
    www.maplepublishers.com

A CIP catalogue record for this title is available from the British Library.

All rights reserved. No part of this book may be reproduced or translated by any form or by any means, electronic or mechanical, including photocopying, recording or by any information storage and retrieval system without written permission from the author.

The views expressed in this work are solely those of the author and do not reflect the opinions of Publishers, and the Publisher hereby disclaims any responsibility for them. This book should not be used as a substitute for the advice of a competent authority, admitted or authorized to advise on the subjects covered.

Contents

Chapter 1 – What is Foster Care? 4

Chapter 2 – What Will Be Different? 15

Chapter 3 – How You Might Feel 25

Chapter 4 – Challenges and Changes 30

Chapter 5 – The Bright Side 37

Chapter 6 – About the Author 48

Chapter 1
What is Foster Care?

What is Foster Care?

Foster care is like finding a safe and cosy shelter during a storm. Sometimes, a child's home might not feel safe or be the right place to stay for a while. This can happen for many reasons, but none of it is the child's fault. That's when foster care steps in to help.

Foster care means living with a foster family. These are kind and caring people who open their homes and hearts to help children feel safe, loved, and looked after. It's like staying with a trusted friend until your birth family is ready to take care of you again. Foster carers are trained to make sure you feel welcome, supported, and comfortable in their home.

Think of it as going on a special journey. Every journey is different, and every family you meet on the way has its own way of making you feel at home. Foster carers want to know what makes you happy, what foods you like, and what activities bring you joy. They might help you go to school, play sports, or try new hobbies. They're there to listen to you, help you solve problems, and cheer you on.

While foster care is a temporary home, it is a very important one. Sometimes, you might feel unsure or have questions, and that's okay! Foster carers, social workers, and other helpers are always there to answer your queries in a simple manner and make sure you're doing well.

Remember, foster care doesn't mean you're alone. It means you're being cared for by people who want to see you thrive, even if they aren't your birth family. No matter where you are, you're special, important, and loved.

New Beginnings Understanding Fostering

What Do Foster Carers Do?

Foster carers have a significant job to do. Let's explore what they do to help you:

1. They Keep You Safe

Foster carers make sure you have a safe and happy place to live. Your new home is like a warm hug—a place where you don't have to worry about anything scary. They work hard to create a cosy, peaceful space where you can feel calm, cared for, and loved.

When you first arrive, everything might feel a little new and different. That's okay! Foster carers are there to guide you and help you settle in. They might teach you fun new routines to help you feel at home, like a bedtime story before you sleep or a special way to set the table for dinner. These little routines are like friendly hugs for your day, making it easier to know what comes next and feel comfortable.

Foster carers also make sure you're safe in every way. They ensure your new room is just right for you—maybe with soft blankets, a nightlight, or even a cuddly teddy bear. Everything they do is to make sure you feel protected and cared for, so you can be yourself and grow.

2. They Take Care of Your Needs

Foster carers will make sure you have everything you need every single day. They work hard to keep you comfy, healthy, and happy, so you can feel at your very best.

Here are some important ways they look after you:

- **Your Own Bed to Sleep In:** They make sure you have your own bed, with fluffy pillows and soft blankets. It's your special place to rest, dream big dreams, and wake up ready for a brand new day.
- **Healthy and Yummy Meals to Eat:** Foster carers prepare delicious meals to keep your tummy full and your body strong. They might even ask you to help pick your favourite foods or teach you how to cook something fun together!

- **Clean Clothes to Wear:** Every morning, you'll have clean, comfy clothes to put on. They might even help you choose your outfits or find shoes that are just right for jumping in puddles or running around the park.

But that's not all! Foster carers also:

- **Help You Learn:** They make sure you get to school on time, where you can learn amazing things and make new friends. If you need help with your homework, they're right there to explain tricky questions or cheer you on as you try your best.
- **Keep You Healthy:** If you're feeling sick or need a check-up, foster carers take you to the doctor to make sure you're okay. They might even give you a spoonful of medicine or a cosy blanket to help you feel better.

3. They Listen and Care About Your Feelings

Sometimes, being in foster care can feel a little confusing, scary, or even sad. That's okay—it's normal to have these feelings. Foster carers understand this and want to help. They are always ready to listen and care about how you feel.

You can talk to them anytime, no matter what you're feeling. Are you happy because something great happened at school? They'll cheer with you! Are you sad or mad and don't know how to explain it? That's okay, too. They'll sit with you, listen carefully, and help you find the words—or they'll just give you a big hug if that's what you need.

If you're feeling upset, foster carers have special ways to help you feel better. They might:

- Sit down with you and talk about what's on your mind
- Offer to do something fun together, like colouring, playing a game, or baking cookies
- Teach you ways to feel calm, like taking deep breaths or snuggling up with a favourite stuffed animal

Your feelings are important, and foster carers want to make sure you know that. Whether you're smiling, laughing, crying, or even feeling grumpy, they're always there for you. They'll help you understand your emotions, make sense of tricky days, and remind you that it's okay to feel however you feel.

With foster carers, you're never alone. They care about you. They believe in you, and they're here to support you every step of the way.

4. They Work with Other People Who Care About You

Foster carers aren't alone! They're part of a team of people who all want to make sure you're safe and happy. This team might include:

Social Workers

Imagine having a friendly helper who's like a guide on a big adventure! That's what a social worker is for children in foster care. First, the social workers spend time getting to know what each child needs to feel safe and happy. Then, a personalised plan is created to support the child in achieving set goals.

Social workers will also check your bedrooms regularly to make sure you have all you need and your needs are met. This is for your benefit, to ensure you are comfortable and well cared for.

Social workers also speak to the child's foster carer and family to make sure everyone is working as a team. Foster carers have their own social worker, too—a supervising social worker. They're like a coach who supports foster carers as they care for children.

Schools

Schools have superheroes too. They're called designated teachers for looked-after children. Their mission is to help kids in foster care shine bright like stars. These teachers monitor the child's progress in class and assist in setting exciting goals for the future. Whether it's becoming an artist, a scientist, or a football player, the designated teacher is there to help kids dream big and reach for the stars!

Health Professionals

Health professionals are like a caring team of doctors and nurses for children in foster care. They make sure every child feels strong, healthy, and ready for anything. A special nurse, called a "looked-after children nurse," checks on the child's health and well-being. Other health professionals work together with the nurse to ensure that the child's needs are met. They also ensure that the child stays active and eats yummy, healthy food.

Psychologists

Sometimes, feelings can feel big and tricky, and that's when a clinical psychologist steps in. They're like feelings detectives who help children understand and express what's going on inside themselves. Support is also offered to families and foster carers, guiding them in working together more effectively to create a stable and nurturing environment. This might involve improving communication, strengthening relationships, and finding positive ways to handle challenges. By offering strategies to manage emotions, resolve conflicts, and build trust, a clinical psychologist helps ensure that everyone involved can support the child's emotional well-being and overall development.

Independent Reviewing Officers

Think of an independent reviewing officer (IRO) as a super-smart organiser who keeps everyone on track. They work with the child, family, and wider team to ensure the child's plan is being followed effectively and progressing smoothly.

This amazing group of people work together to make sure every child in foster care is surrounded by love, care, and support. Together, they're like a team of superheroes, each with their own special power, all working to help children grow and thrive!

Foster carers share updates with a dedicated team of professionals, including social workers, teachers, therapists, and clinical psychologists.

This ensures that everyone involved in the child's care is aware of their emotional state, progress, and the relevant support they may need. By working together, these individuals can provide the right guidance, resources, and encouragement to help the child thrive.

5. They Help You Stay Connected

Even though you're not living with your birth family right now, that doesn't mean you stop caring about each other. Foster carers understand how much your family means to you and want to help you stay connected with them in safe and loving ways.

There are lots of ways foster carers can help you keep in touch:

- **Visiting Your Family:** They might take you to see your family so you can spend time together. Maybe you'll share stories, play games, or even give them a big hug!
- **Talking to Them on the Phone:** If visiting isn't possible, you can call your family on the phone. Hearing their voices can feel like a warm hug from far away.
- **Sending Letters, Drawings, or Pictures:** Do you love drawing or writing? Foster carers can help you create special messages to send to your family, like a drawing of your favourite animal or a picture of you smiling. These little surprises can help you feel close, even when you're apart.

Foster carers know that your family is a very special part of your life. So, they'll work hard to make sure you can share happy moments and stay connected with your family. Whether it's a quick phone call to say hello or a visit where you get to laugh and play together, your foster carers will help you feel loved and supported by everyone who's important to you.

You're surrounded by people who care about you—your foster carers, your family, and so many others. Together, they make sure you always feel special and loved.

New Beginnings Understanding Fostering

6. They Respect Your Story

Your life is special, like a story filled with unique memories, favourite things, and traditions that are all about you. Foster carers want to learn about your story and make sure you feel valued and loved just the way you are.

They'll take the time to understand what matters most to you, such as:

- **Your Favourite Foods:** Do you have a meal that makes you feel happy or reminds you of home? Maybe it's spaghetti, pancakes, or a yummy soup. Foster carers will try to include your favourite foods so that your meals feel comforting and special. They might even ask you to help in the kitchen and share how it's made!
- **Holidays and Traditions You Celebrate:** Every family has its own way of celebrating holidays or special days. Whether it is lighting candles, singing songs, or making a certain dish, foster carers will listen and learn about what's important to you. They'll do their best to include your traditions so you feel right at home, even during special times of the year.
- **The People, Places, and Memories That Make You Feel at Home:** Maybe you have a favourite park where you loved to play, a song that reminds you of someone special, or a story about a family trip. Foster carers will listen to these memories because they're part of your story—and your story is what makes you, you!

Foster carers know that everyone's story is different and that those differences are what make you unique. They'll do their best to make you feel comfortable, understood, and valued every single day. With them, you'll always have a place where your story is celebrated.

A Temporary Home, A Helping Hand

The most important thing to remember is that foster carers are here to help. They have a big, caring job: to make sure you're safe, loved, and have everything you need while your birth family works on becoming a safe and happy place for you to return to, if and when the time is right.

Foster care isn't forever—it's more like a bridge. A bridge helps you get from one place to another safely, and that's exactly what foster carers do for you. They are there to give you a cosy, caring home for now, helping you feel strong and supported while everyone works together to figure out what's best for your future.

While you're with foster carers, they will:

- Make sure you have everything you need, like a comfy bed, yummy food, and clothes that fit just right
- Be there to cheer you on, whether it's at school, on the playground, or when you're trying something new
- Listen to your feelings and help you feel safe and cared for

Even though foster care is a temporary part of your life, it is still an important chapter in your story. Foster carers are there to help you along the way, making sure you know that you're special, loved, and never alone.

Remember, this bridge isn't one you have to cross by yourself. Foster carers, your family, and so many others are here to hold your hand and help you move forward to the next part of your journey—one step at a time.

Chapter 2
What Will Be Different?

When You Move to a Foster Home

When you go to live with foster carers, some things might be different from what you are used to. But don't worry—these changes are meant to help you feel safe and cared for. Let's explore what might be new:

1. A New Place to Call Home

When you arrive at your foster home, you'll have a special new place to call your own. Here you will also have your own room. It might look different from the room you had before, but it's your space to make as cosy and special as you like.

You can decorate it with all your favourite things—maybe your stuffed animals, colourful drawings, or a soft blanket that feels just right. You might even pick a spot for a favourite toy or hang up a picture that makes you smile. Little by little, your new room will start to feel more like your place.

The house itself might feel new and different, too. Maybe it smells like cookies baking in the kitchen or fresh flowers on the table. The furniture might be arranged in ways you're not used to, or the house could be in a neighbourhood with new parks and streets to explore.

It's okay to feel curious, excited, or even a little nervous about all these changes. New places can take time to feel like home, and that's perfectly normal. Your foster carers will help you get to know your surroundings, and they'll make sure you feel welcome, safe, and comfortable.

Soon, you might find little things that make you smile, like a cosy corner to read in, a sunny window to look out of, or a favourite chair to curl up on. Over time, this new house will feel more and more familiar—like a home where you can rest, play, and be yourself.

2. New Routines

Every family has its own special way of doing things. When you move into your foster home, you might notice that your foster family has routines that are a little different from what you're used to. That's okay—new routines can feel strange at first, but they're like a friendly guide to help you feel settled and safe.

For example:

- **Meal Times:** Your foster family might have set times for meals, like breakfast at the table every morning or dinner together in the evening. They might even have fun traditions, like a "pizza night".
- **Bedtime Routines:** Bedtime might include brushing your teeth in a certain order, picking out pyjamas, or reading a story together. Maybe your foster carer will tuck you in and leave a nightlight on if you like. These routines help you feel calm and cosy before going to sleep.
- **Helping Out with Chores:** You might have new responsibilities, like feeding a pet, tidying your room, or setting the table. Helping with chores can be a fun way to be part of the family team!

Your foster family might also celebrate holidays or traditions that are new to you. Maybe they bake cookies for a special occasion, decorate the house in a certain way, or play fun games during a family celebration. These moments can be exciting and are a great way to learn about the people you're living with.

New Beginnings Understanding Fostering

It's okay to have questions if you're not sure how things work. Your foster carers are always happy to help you understand and make sure you feel safe and comfortable.

Over time, these new routines can start to feel familiar and even fun. They're like little pieces of a puzzle that fit together to create a home full of love, laughter, and care just for you.

3. New Foods to Try

One of the exciting benefits about living with a foster family is that you might get to try foods that are new to you. Foster carers might cook dishes that smell, look, or taste different from what you're used to eating, and that's okay. Trying new foods can be like going on a little adventure right at the dinner table!

Imagine tasting a soup with spices that warm you up, biting into a vegetable you've never seen before, or trying a dessert that's sweet and gooey in just the right way. Some new foods might become your favourites, while others might make you scrunch up your nose—and that's okay, too!

If there are foods you already know you love, like pizza, mac & cheese, or fruit, let your foster carers know. They'll be happy to include those in your meals. If there's something you don't like or are nervous to try, you can tell them that, too. They'll listen and do their best to make sure you're happy and well-fed.

Sometimes, trying new foods can feel a little scary, but foster carers will be there to encourage you. They might say something like, "Just one little bite, and if you don't like it, that's okay!" Over time, you might surprise yourself by discovering how much you enjoy these new tastes.

Remember, meal times are about more than just food—they're a chance to sit together, share stories, and laugh. Whether you're eating something familiar or trying something new, your foster carers will make sure every meal is made with love, just for you.

4. New People in Your Life

When you move into your foster home, you'll meet new people who are excited to get to know you. These might include your foster carer, their family, and maybe even other children who live there. It's okay if it takes time to feel comfortable with them—getting to know new people is like planting a flower. It starts small, but with care, it can grow into something wonderful.

Your foster carers will help you feel welcome in their home. They might introduce you to everyone, show you around the house, and even share fun aspects about their family, like favourite games to play or stories about their pets. If there are other children living there, they might invite you to play or share their toys with you.

In addition to your foster family, you'll also see other important adults who are part of your support team. These people are there to make sure you're happy, healthy, and cared for.

You'll also see adults like social workers, teachers, and maybe doctors more often. These people are part of your support team. Their job is to check in and make sure you're doing well.

It's okay to feel shy or unsure around new people at first. Remember, all of these people are here to care about you and make sure you're okay. Over time, they'll become part of the team that helps you feel supported and loved.

With so many caring people around you, you'll never be alone. They're all working together to make sure you feel safe, happy, and ready to explore everything life has to offer.

5. Staying in Touch with Your Birth Family

Even though you're living in foster care, your birth family is still very important to you, and you can still stay connected with them. Your foster carers understand how special your family is, and they will do everything they can to help you stay in touch—if it's safe to do so.

Here are some of the ways you might stay in touch with your family:

- **Visiting Your Family:** If it's safe, you might get to visit your parents, siblings, or other family members. These visits can be a chance to spend time together, share stories, or even play games.
- **Talking on the Phone or Video Calls:** Sometimes, you might talk to your family on the phone or even see them on a video call. Hearing their voices or seeing their faces can help you feel close, even when you're apart.
- **Writing Letters or Drawing Pictures:** You might also send letters, drawings, or pictures to your family. Sharing your artwork, telling them about your day, or just saying hello can help you stay connected in a meaningful way.

Sometimes, visits with your family might feel exciting because you're happy to see them, or they might feel confusing if you're not sure what to expect. It's also okay if visits feel a little hard, because your feelings are important. You might miss your family, feel nervous, or not know exactly what to say. All of these feelings are perfectly normal.

Your foster carer and social worker are there to help you talk about your feelings. They're great listeners and can help you understand what's going on or help you feel better if you're feeling worried. They're always there to support you, whether you're excited to see your family or you need help talking through tough feelings.

Staying in touch with your birth family is just one way that you're still connected to them, and your foster carers will help you keep that connection strong and safe.

6. School and Friends

Even though you're living in foster care, you'll still go to school—just like before. You might stay at your old school, where you already know the teachers and some friends, or you might start at a new school. Starting somewhere new can feel a little scary at first, but it's also a chance to meet new people and make new friends!

At a new school, you'll have teachers who are excited to get to know you and help you learn and grow. They'll create a supportive environment where you feel safe, and they'll encourage you to do your best in every subject. You'll also have opportunities to join activities like sports teams, art clubs, or music classes, where you can explore new interests and talents.

If you feel nervous about starting at a new school, that's completely okay. Talk to your foster carer or your teacher—they'll be there to help you every step of the way. They'll listen to your worries and provide you with the tools you need to feel comfortable.

Your foster carer might help you:

- Get school supplies like a new backpack, pencils, or a lunchbox
- Practise what to say when making new friends or starting conversations
- Learn about the school's rules, schedule, or special events, so you know what to expect

They'll also help you stay connected with old friends if that's important to you. Whether it's calling or sending messages, they'll make sure you feel supported even when you're apart from your old school friends.

Making friends at a new school can be exciting, but it can also take time. Be patient with yourself, and remember—it's okay to feel shy at first. Slowly, you'll find friends who share your interests and who support you just like a big family.

Your foster carers are right there with you, cheering you on as you take this new step toward discovering who you are and all the amazing things you can do.

7. Adjusting to the Changes

At first, all these changes might feel like a lot. You're in a new home, meeting new people, and trying new things. It's okay to feel a bit overwhelmed or miss the things you're used to, like your birth family, old friends, or your favourite routines. These feelings are completely normal, and it's important to remember that you don't have to figure everything out right away.

Sometimes, change can bring new adventures and experiences that you might enjoy. You might discover a new hobby, a new favourite food, or a new friend. That's exciting! But it's also okay to feel unsure, sad, or confused, too. All of those feelings are part of the process of adjusting to your new life.

Here are some tips to help make the transition easier:

- **Ask Questions:** If something is confusing or you don't understand how something works, don't be afraid to ask questions to your foster carer, social worker, or even a teacher. They're there to help answer your questions and make sure you feel safe and comfortable. No question is too small!

- **Be Patient with Yourself:** Getting used to new places and people takes time. It's okay if you don't feel completely comfortable right away. You might need time to settle into your new room, get to know your foster carers, or feel confident in your new school. Be kind to yourself as you make these changes.

- **Talk About Your Feelings:** Sometimes, your feelings can be hard to understand, especially when everything feels new or different. Talking to someone you trust, like your foster carer, social worker, or even a friend, can help. They'll listen to how you're feeling and help you work through it. You don't have to keep your feelings inside—you're not alone!

Over time, you'll start to feel more at home in your new space. The new routines, the new faces, and all the little changes will start to feel familiar. With each day, you'll find your rhythm, and things will start to feel more like they're meant to be.

Remember, you're doing the best you can, and that's enough. You're stronger than you know, and you'll get through this with the support of all the people who care about you.

Remember: You're Not Alone

It's important to remember that **you're not alone**. Many children have lived with foster families, and even though the changes might seem big at first, they've found ways to adjust and make the most of their new lives. Just like them, you have people around you who care about you and want to help you through this journey.

Your **foster carers** are there to make you feel safe and supported in your new home. They want to get to know you, understand what makes you happy, and help you feel comfortable. You can count on them to listen to you, help you with your homework, and give you a hug when you need one.

You also have a **social worker** who's there to check in on how you're doing. They're like a guide who will help you understand what's happening and support you through any tough moments.

At school, your **teachers** are there to help you learn new things and to make sure you're feeling okay while you're at school. They'll encourage you, help you with lessons, and listen to your thoughts and ideas.

And don't forget about your **new friends!** Whether you meet them at school, in your foster home, or through activities, new friends can be an amazing source of support. They can help you feel more at home and remind you that you have someone to laugh with, talk to, and share stories with.

Change can be hard, especially when everything around you is new. But remember, **change can also bring new opportunities**—like new things to try, new people to meet, and new experiences that can help you grow. Take one step at a time. You don't need to have all the answers right away. Each day is a fresh start, and with each new day, you'll feel a little bit more settled.

No matter what, you have a **team** of people who are cheering you on and want you to feel safe, supported, and loved. So, when you feel nervous or unsure, remember: You are not alone. You've got a group of caring people ready to help you through each step of the way.

Chapter 3
How You Might Feel

It's Okay to Feel a Mix of Emotions

Moving into foster care can bring up a lot of different feelings. One moment, you might feel happy and excited about the new things you're trying, like making new friends or exploring your new home. But the next moment, you might feel sad or confused, missing your old home or the people you used to live with. **That's completely normal!**

It's okay to have a mix of emotions. Sometimes, our feelings can change quickly, and that's just a part of adjusting to something new. You might feel the following:

1. Confused

You might feel confused about why you're living with a foster family. Questions like "Why can't I stay with my birth family?" or "How long will I be here?" might pop into your head.

This is a normal feeling. It's okay to ask questions about what's happening. Your foster carers or social worker can provide answers to you in a way that makes sense. Understanding your situation might not take away all the confusion, but it can help you feel a little more in control.

2. Sad

It's natural to feel sad when you're apart from your birth family, your home, or the way things used to be. Even if things weren't perfect, it's okay to miss the people and places you know.

If you're feeling sad, try these ideas:
- Talk to someone you trust. This could be your foster carer, teacher, social worker, IRO or anyone you feel comfortable with.
- Do something you enjoy, like drawing, reading, or playing outside.
- Remember, it's okay to cry. Showing your feelings can help you feel better.

3. Angry

You might feel angry about being in foster care. Thoughts like "Why did this happen to me?" or feelings of frustration about how much your life has changed are normal.

It's important to let out your anger in ways that are healthy. Here's how:

- Talk about your feelings with someone who understands. This could be your foster carer or anyone you feel comfortable with.
- Write about your emotions in a journal/diary.
- Do something active, like dancing, jumping on a trampoline, going for a bike ride, or playing a sport.

Remember, it's okay to feel angry, but try not to let it make you act in ways that might hurt yourself or others.

4. Scared or Nervous

A new home, new people, and new routines can feel scary. You might worry about what's going to happen next or if you'll fit in with your foster family.

Here are some tips to feel less scared:
- Ask your foster carer or social worker to explain what's happening.

- Take it one day at a time. Things might feel easier as you get used to your new home.
- Remember, your foster carers want you to feel safe and cared for.

5. Happy or Curious

It's okay to feel happy or curious about your new home. Maybe you're excited to try new things, meet new people, or explore a different environment. Feeling happy doesn't mean you've forgotten your birth family—it just means you're finding moments of joy in your new situation.

6. Feeling Stuck Between Two Worlds

Sometimes, you might feel caught between your birth family and your foster family. You might love both, or you might feel loyal to one and unsure about the other.

This is quite a common feeling. It's okay to care about both families and to have mixed emotions about your situation. You can talk about these feelings with someone you trust, like your social worker or foster carer.

7. Feeling Different

You might feel like you're different from other kids because you're in foster care. You might wonder: "Will people treat me differently?" or "Do I have to tell others about my situation?"

8. Relieved or Hopeful

Even though you might feel sad or confused sometimes, you might also feel relief, like knowing you're in a safe place or having a chance to start fresh.

Feelings are not right or wrong—they're just how you feel, and all feelings are okay.

Talking about how you feel can help you understand your emotions better. It's a way to make sense of what's going on inside. You might want to talk to your **foster carer** or **social worker** about how you're feeling. They're there to listen and help you work through your emotions. Maybe you want to draw a picture of how you feel, write it down in a journal, or talk it out with a trusted adult.

You don't have to figure out your feelings all on your own. There are people who want to help you, and it's always okay to share how you feel. Talking about your emotions can make them easier to understand and help you feel better.

Remember, feeling happy, sad, angry, or even confused is part of being human.

You are not alone in your feelings, and there are many people around you who want to help you feel better. Take your time to adjust, and always know it's okay to express how you're feeling. Being in foster care doesn't define who you are. You are still you, with your own personality, talents, and dreams. It's up to you who you tell about your situation.

9. What to Do When Emotions Feel Overwhelming

Some feelings can be hard to handle, but there are ways to manage them:

- **Talk:** Sharing your feelings with someone you trust can help you feel less alone.
- **Create:** Draw, write, or make something that expresses how you feel.
- **Relax:** Try deep breathing, listening to music, or spending time in nature.
- **Ask for Help:** If your feelings are too difficult to handle on your own, let your foster carer or social worker know.

You Are Not Alone

Whatever you're feeling, remember that it's okay to feel that way. There are people around you—like your foster carers, social workers, and teachers—who care about you and want to help. You don't have to go through this alone.

Your emotions are an important part of your story, and sharing them can help you feel stronger and more understood. No matter how you feel, you are loved, cared for, and supported.

Chapter 4
Challenges and Changes

Moving into foster care is a big change, and it's okay if it feels hard at first. Change can make you feel excited and worried all at once, and that's perfectly normal. Sometimes, when everything around you is new or different, it can feel like you're walking through a fog not knowing what is on the other side. But remember, it's also a chance to grow, discover new things, and meet people who care about you.

In this chapter, we'll explore some of the feelings and situations you might experience. With these tips, you'll feel more ready to face them, knowing you're not alone and there's always help when you need it.

1. Missing Your Birth Family

When you move into foster care, you may feel like you've left behind part of your world. Missing your birth family is a normal and natural feeling, even if things at home were hard. Sometimes, you might miss your parents, siblings, or even pets. It's okay to feel sad or confused, and it's important to understand that those feelings are part of adjusting to a big change.

How to Cope:

When you miss your family, it helps to keep the happy memories alive. You could create a memory book with pictures, drawings, or mementos from happy times you've shared. You may also want to write letters or draw pictures to send to them. Doing things that remind you of the good times helps keep you connected, even if you're apart.

New Beginnings Understanding Fostering

If you're feeling overwhelmed by missing them, talk to your foster carer or social worker. They understand what you're going through and will listen to you. Remember, foster care isn't forever, and it's often a temporary place where you can stay safe while your family works on making things better. Many children return to their families once things are safe, and some might even find new ways to stay connected.

2. Getting Used to New Rules

Every family has its own set of rules, and when you move into a new foster family, you'll need to learn their rules. The rules might be different from what you're used to at home. For example, maybe your bedtime is earlier or later, or there might be new chores to do, like setting the table or feeding a pet. It's normal to feel frustrated at first, especially when things feel unfamiliar.

How to Cope:

Take your time learning the rules. It's okay to ask questions if something isn't clear. "Why do we have to go to bed so early?" or "How should I clean my room?" These are good questions to ask your foster carers. They will help you understand the reasons behind the rules, and they will make sure you feel comfortable.

Remember, these rules are there to help everyone in the house stay safe, happy, and organised. If a rule feels tough to follow, talk to your foster carers. They'll help you figure out how to manage and make it easier for you.

3. Feeling Like You Don't Belong

When you first arrive at your foster home, you might feel like you're an outsider. It's normal to feel different or like you don't quite fit in yet. Sometimes, the people in your foster family may seem like strangers, and the house may feel unfamiliar.

How to Cope:

Give yourself time to adjust. It's okay if you don't feel at home right away. Getting to know your foster carers and their family will take time, and that's perfectly fine. You might start with small things, like telling them about your favourite games, books, or hobbies. Over time, you'll start to feel more connected. It's also important to remember that your feelings are valid—you belong in your foster home just as much as anyone else.

4. Meeting New People

Along with your foster family, you may meet new people like social workers, teachers, doctors, IRO, or even other children in your foster family. These people are there to help you, but meeting so many new faces can feel overwhelming. It might be hard to trust them at first, or you might feel shy.

How to Cope:

Take things slow and don't feel pressured to share everything about yourself right away. Getting to know someone can take time, and it's okay to build trust step by step. If you feel nervous, talk to someone who you feel comfortable with, like your foster carer. They'll help you feel safe and give you the space you need to warm up to new people. Remember, these new people are here to support you and help you thrive.

5. Moving Schools

Sometimes, being in foster care means that you'll change schools. This can be a really big change, especially if you have to leave behind your old friends and teachers. Starting at a new school may feel like a fresh start, but it can also be intimidating.

How to Cope:

It's okay to feel nervous about going to a new school. Talk to your foster carer or teacher about how you're feeling—they're there to help you settle in. Don't feel like you have to make new friends right away; just be yourself, and remember that people will like you for who you are. Try focusing on things that make school fun, like your favourite subjects, activities, or friends you may meet later. It will take time, but soon enough, you'll start to feel more comfortable.

6. Feeling Like You're Stuck in the Middle

Sometimes, when you're living in foster care, it can feel like you're stuck between two families—your birth family and your foster family. You might love both, and it can feel confusing when you feel torn between them.

How to Cope:

It's okay to care about both your birth family and your foster family. You don't have to choose between them. Both are important, and it's possible to love and respect both families in different ways. Talk to someone you trust and feel comfortable with, like your social worker or foster carer, about how you're feeling. They can help you navigate these mixed emotions. Focus on being kind to yourself and allowing yourself to love both families for the unique roles they each play in your life.

7. Dealing with Big Feelings

You might have days when you feel lots of big emotions at once. You might feel sad, angry, happy, or confused. It's okay to feel all of these emotions. In fact, it's totally normal to have mixed emotions during a big change. But when those emotions feel too overwhelming, it's important to know how to cope.

New Beginnings Understanding Fostering

How to Cope:

Take a deep breath, and think of ways to express how you're feeling. You could draw a picture, write in a journal, or talk to a trusted adult about your emotions. Sometimes, it helps to focus on something that calms you down, like a hobby, listening to music, or reading a favourite book. If you ever feel like your feelings are too big to handle alone, it's okay to ask for help. You don't have to carry the weight of your emotions by yourself.

8. Looking Forward

Even though foster care might feel hard right now, it can also open up new opportunities. As you adjust to this change, you might discover new strengths and interests you never knew you had.

How to Cope:

Focus on the things that make you happy—whether it's a new hobby, new friends, or exciting things you learn at school. Life in foster care is a chance to grow, and though it might feel difficult, it's also a time to learn more about yourself. New experiences can bring new strengths, so be open to trying new things.

You Are Not Alone

Through all the challenges, remember that you are never alone. You have a team of people around you who care about you. Your foster carers, social worker, teachers, and even new friends are there to support you, every step of the way. They want you to feel safe, loved, and supported, no matter what.

Foster care is one part of your life story. No matter how difficult it seems at times, each challenge you face is helping you grow stronger. You are brave. You are important, and you have people who want to help you succeed. So, take it one day at a time, and know that you are never alone on this journey.

Chapter 5
The Bright Side

Foster care can feel like a big change, and it's natural to have some mixed feelings about it. But, just like when you plant a seed and it grows into something wonderful, foster care has the potential to bring out new strengths, new experiences, and new opportunities for you. Although it might feel tough sometimes, there are so many amazing things you can look forward to, and special moments you can create with the people around you. Let's dive deeper into it and see how you'll benefit from foster care:

1. A Safe and Caring Environment

The heart of foster care is about giving you a safe place to live, a place where you feel like you belong. Your foster carers work really hard to make sure you're safe, comfortable, and loved. Their job is to create an environment where you can grow, feel secure, and thrive. Even if everything around you feels new and different, your foster carers want to help you feel at home.

Here's how your foster home can provide that:
- **A Cosy Room Just for You**: It might not seem like much at first but having a room that's just yours can make a huge difference. This space is where you can unwind, decorate with your favourite things, and keep your personal belongings safe.
- **Tasty and Healthy Meals**: Your foster carers are dedicated to making sure you have enough food to eat, and that it's nutritious and good for you. Imagine having meals made with care, maybe even trying new dishes that are delicious and fun!

- **Time with People Who Care About You**: Living in foster care means you'll be surrounded by people who care about you—whether it's your foster carers, their family, or even pets that are there to brighten your day. They will make sure you feel safe and cared for, just like family.

2. New People Who Care About You

In foster care, you'll meet many people whose job it is to help you, support you, and make sure you're okay. These new people are part of your team, and their goal is to help you grow and succeed.

Some of the people you'll meet include:

- **Foster Carers**: They are your home base. They open their doors and hearts to you, providing love and guidance. They might not be your birth family, but they'll be there for you every step of the way, helping you navigate new routines and making you feel welcome.
- **Social Workers**: These adults check in on you to make sure you're doing well and feeling safe. Social workers are there to listen to your concerns, answer your questions, and make sure your needs are met.
- **Teachers**: These adults are there to help you with learning and schoolwork, but they also want to make sure you're happy and doing well emotionally. If you're feeling nervous or having a hard time with something, they are there to lend a ear or give advice.

Each one of these people is there to help you succeed. They are part of your team and want to make sure you are safe, supported, and cared for.

3. Learning New Things

Foster care isn't just about adjusting to new people and places—it's also an exciting time to learn new things. Whether it's discovering a new hobby, trying a fun activity, or learning useful life skills, foster care can open doors to experiences you might not have expected.

Here's what you might learn:
- **Hobbies and Interests:** You might get the chance to try something fun like painting, playing an instrument, or baking your favourite cookies. Foster care gives you the time and space to explore things you enjoy and discover new talents.
- **Family Outings:** Your foster carers might take you to new places like parks, zoos, museums, or even trips to new cities. These are experiences that can be exciting and fun, and they can also help you learn about the world around you.
- **Life Skills:** Living with a foster family is also about learning how to take care of yourself and your home. You might learn how to help cook a meal, organise your room, or take care of pets. These skills will stay with you as you grow.

Learning new activities is an exciting part of being in foster care, and every new experience helps you discover even more about what you love and what you're good at.

4. Making Happy Memories

Even though foster care can be full of challenges, it also has the potential to create happy memories. These special moments might not happen every day but, when they do, they help make your time in foster care a little brighter.

Here are some memories you might make:
- **Movie Nights and Game Nights**: Imagine cosying up on the couch for a movie night with your foster family, or having a fun game night where everyone laughs and enjoys each other's company. These little moments can make you feel loved and happy.

New Beginnings Understanding Fostering

- **Celebrations and Traditions**: Holidays, birthdays, and special events are important occasions to create memories. You might have new traditions with your foster family or celebrate holidays in ways you've never experienced before.
- **Making New Friends**: You'll meet new friends in school or in the neighbourhood. Sometimes, friendships blossom when you least expect them, and they can be a bright part of your foster care experience.

These happy memories can help you get through tough moments and show you that, even during challenges, there is joy to be found.

5. Building Confidence

Being in foster care will help you grow, and you might not even realise just how strong and capable you are becoming. Every time you face something new or challenging, you build your confidence and resilience.

As you adjust to new routines, try new activities, or share how you're feeling, you'll discover just how much you're growing emotionally and mentally. Here's how you might see your confidence grow:

- **Handling Tough Situations**: At first, starting a new school or meeting new people might seem scary, but over time, you'll handle those situations with more confidence. You might start feeling more comfortable speaking up in class or asking for help when you need it.
- **Expressing Yourself**: Talking about your feelings can sometimes be hard, but with time, you'll get better at expressing yourself and sharing what's on your mind. Whether it's through talking, drawing, or journalling, you'll learn how to communicate what you're feeling.
- **Trying New Things**: Trying new hobbies or making new friends might feel intimidating at first, but each time you try something new, you gain more confidence. And as you succeed

at these things, you'll feel proud of yourself for growing and learning.

- **Feeling Proud**: As you face challenges and grow, you'll feel a sense of accomplishment. That feeling of pride is an important part of building your confidence. Whether it's handling a tough day or trying something you thought you couldn't do, each small victory matters.

Building confidence is a process and every step you take— no matter how small—helps you grow stronger.

6. Staying Connected to Your Roots

One of the most important things about foster care is that it doesn't mean you have to forget about your birth family. If it's safe, your foster carers and social worker will help you stay in touch with your family, whether it's through phone calls, video chats, or visits.

Even if you can't see them as much as you would like, there are other ways to stay connected:

- **Sending Drawings and Letters:** You might write letters or draw pictures for your birth family to keep them updated on your life. These small gestures can show that you care about them and want to keep the bond alive.
- **Sharing Happy Memories:** Talking about the good times you've had with your birth family can help you stay connected to your past, even while you live with your foster family.
- **Keeping Special Items:** If you have special photos or items that remind you of your birth family, keep them in a safe place. These can help you feel connected, even if you're living in a new home.

Remember, your foster family and your birth family both play important roles in your life, and staying connected to both can help you feel whole.

7. Looking Ahead

Foster care is just one chapter in your journey, and it's helping you grow in ways that will prepare you for the future. Every new experience and challenge you face is a step towards becoming the person you're meant to be.

This time in foster care will help you:
- **Become stronger emotionally and mentally,** learning how to face tough situations with resilience and confidence
- **Learn life skills** that will help you as you get older, like managing your time, taking care of yourself, and building healthy relationships
- **Build friendships** that will last, and discover talents you might not have known you had
- **Get ready for the future** by building a foundation of love, care, and support that will help you succeed in everything you do

The future is full of endless possibilities, and foster care is one of the steps that will help you get there.

8. You Deserve to Be Happy

Sometimes, you might feel like it's not okay to enjoy the good things about your life in foster care. You might feel like you're betraying your birth family if you're happy or having fun. But the truth is: **You deserve to be happy.** It's okay to smile, laugh, and enjoy yourself while you're in foster care.

Being happy doesn't mean you've forgotten your birth family. It just means you're taking care of yourself and finding joy in the present moment. You're allowed to have fun and experience good things in life, no matter where you are.

Conclusion: You Are Brave and Resilient

Foster care is just one chapter in your life, but it's a special one full of courage, growth, and discovery. You are stronger than you realise, and every challenge you face makes you more resilient.

Remember, you are never alone. You have a team of people who care about you and want to see you succeed.

So, keep going. Keep learning. Keep growing. Your future is full of amazing possibilities, and you have everything you need to succeed.

You are loved. You are important. You are brave.

The World Needs Your Light

You are brave, important, and capable of amazing things. Every challenge you've faced has made you stronger, and you are capable of achieving incredible milestones as you continue on your journey. The world is a better place because of you. You have something special that only you can give.

As you go forward, remember that each step is part of something bigger. The future is waiting for you, full of hope and endless opportunities. You might not know exactly what comes next, and that's okay—what matters is that you're moving towards something wonderful. Every time you take a step forward, no matter how big or small, you are making the world a little brighter.

Final Note: The Beginning

Whenever you feel unsure or need help, don't hesitate to ask. There is always someone who is ready to listen to you, support you, and care for you. You are never alone on this journey, and there is always someone waiting to offer you a helping hand, a kind word, or a listening ear.

Always remember:

- **You are loved**—deeply, truly, and always.
- **You are valued**—your thoughts, your feelings, and your presence are important.
- **You are never alone**—there is a team of people who care about you and will support you no matter where your journey takes you.

This is just the beginning of your incredible adventure. Wherever your path leads, remember that you are strong, brave, and capable of achieving amazing things. Keep going, and don't forget that the future is waiting for you to shine.

The beginning of your story is now, and it's full of endless possibilities.

About the Author

Saba Asghar is a passionate foster carer with many years of experience providing love, care, and stability to children from diverse backgrounds, each with their own unique needs and stories. Over the years, Saba has supported children through a variety of placements, from short-term and respite care to long-term support.

Through these experiences, Saba has witnessed firsthand the healing power of love and kindness, and she has found the work of fostering to be incredibly fulfilling. It has not only helped children heal, grow, and thrive but has also transformed Saba deeply. By opening her heart and home, Saba has gained new perspectives and learned invaluable lessons about resilience, empathy, and the importance of community.

Saba hopes that this book will not only provide comfort and inspiration to young readers and those who care for them but also serve as an eye-opener for others. Through sharing her experiences, Saba wants to raise awareness about the foster care system and highlight the difference that love, support, and understanding can make in the lives of children in care.

In addition to fostering, Saba has recently discovered a passion for writing, and she hopes this book is just the first of many. When not caring for children or writing, Saba enjoys hiking and spending time in nature, finding peace and inspiration in the outdoors. Travelling is another passion, as it brings new perspectives and experiences that enrich Saba's life and work.

www.ingramcontent.com/pod-product-compliance
Lightning Source LLC
Chambersburg PA
CBHW041228070526
44584CB00006B/330